D1360360

Sheep

by Robin Nelson

first step nonfiction

Lerner Publications Company · Minneapolis

What lives on a farm?

Sheep live on a farm.

A female sheep is a **ewe**.

A male sheep is a **ram**.

Some sheep have horns.

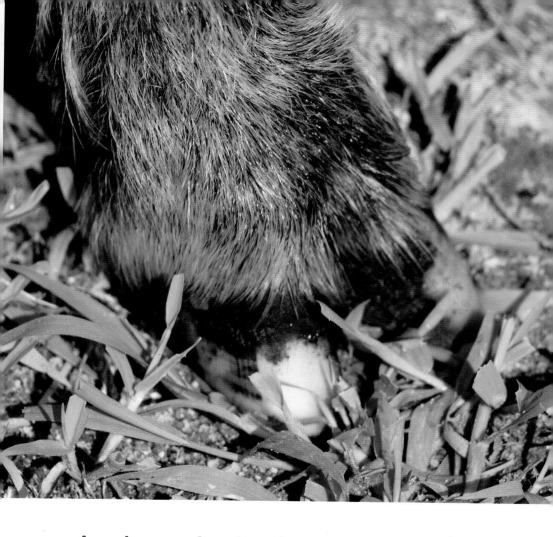

A sheep's foot is called a
hoof.

Sheep eat grass, hay, and oats.

Sheep drink a lot of water.

A baby sheep drinks its
mother's milk.

A baby sheep is called a **lamb**.

Sheep are covered with wool.

The wool keeps them dry and warm.

Every spring, the farmer clips
off the sheep's wool.

This is called **shearing**.

Sheep give us warm wool
for clothes.

It is fun to see sheep on
the farm!

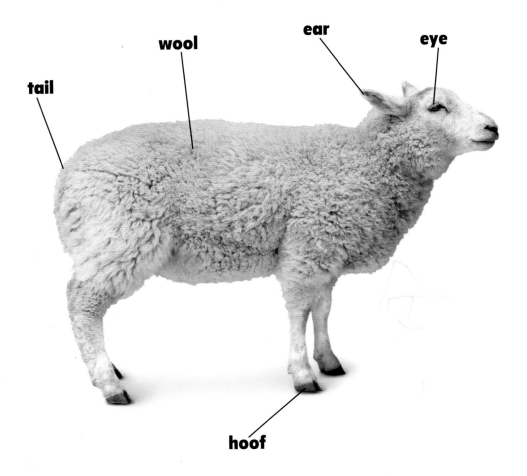

tail

wool

ear

eye

hoof

Parts of a Sheep

There are many different kinds of sheep. Sheep can be many different colors—white, black, or brown.

Some sheep have long curved horns. Sometimes only the ram has horns, and sometimes both the ram and ewe have horns. Many kinds of sheep have no horns at all.

Sheep Facts

 A group of sheep are called a flock.

 A lamb knows its mother by the sound she makes.

 Clothes made out of sheep's wool stay cool in the summer and warm in the winter.

 Texas has the most sheep in the United States.

 Farmers shear a sheep's wool coat in one big piece.

Farmers have to shear a sheep's coat very quickly. They can do it in about five minutes!

A sheep's horns are hollow. That means there is nothing inside of them.

You can guess a sheep's age by looking at its teeth. Long means young, and short means old.

Glossary

 ewe – a female sheep

 hoof – a sheep's foot

 lamb – a baby sheep

 ram – a male sheep

 shearing – cutting off a sheep's wool